rst

e for

29. SEP. 1995	28. NOV 1998	
29. NOV. 1996		
ILL/SBR		
14/2/97		DISCARDED
14. 3. 97.		
20. JUN. 1997		
9-2-00		

Policy

D0101061

University of Brighton 1993

British Library Cataloguing-in-Publication Data.
A catalogue record for this book is available from the British Library.

Users first: the real challenge for community care
Edited by Valerie Williamson
© University of Brighton, 1993
ISBN 1 871966 91 4

Health and Social Policy Research Centre
University of Brighton
Falmer
Brighton
BN1 9PH
Telephone 0273 600900
Facsimile 0273 643473

Contents

Foreword

The papers which follow report on the proceedings of the Brian Hamilton-Cramp Day Conference which took place in June 1992. The conference was organised by staff from the Department of Community Studies at the University of Brighton as a tribute to the former Head of Department who died in May 1991. A fund set up in his memory was utilized on this occasion to enable users of services to participate in the conference. Of the eighty people attending a considerable proportion were users, and this added an important dimension to the discussion groups.

We wish to acknowledge our thanks to friends and colleagues from local statutory and voluntary organisations who gave their time to lead the workshop groups, ensuring a firm practice orientation to the discussions. Only infrequently do users and providers come together in this way. But these were not 'them and us' debates. They were an endeavour to identify and explore issues which are fundamental to the quality of the lives of service users.

A clear theme which came from the conference speakers and from the discussion groups was that strategies for user participation must be built into the fabric of Community Care. Users of services need to be involved in the planning of structures, the implementation and evaluation of services, and in the training of staff. If they are not, then user participation will be one of the first items to be pushed from the agenda when resource constraints send planners and providers into retreat.

I express my personal thanks to Valerie Williamson for editing this publication, and to the staff of the department for compiling the workshop reports. The timely messages of the conference may now be heard by a wider audience.

Tony Hadley
Department of Community Studies
University of Brighton
March 1993

1 Users first: from policy to practice

Valerie Williamson, Director
Health and Social Policy Research Centre
University of Brighton

Policy background

In April 1993 major changes are due to take place in the field of community care. Multi disciplinary needs assessment is to precede the compilation of packages of care, which will then be 'purchased' from a wide range of potential statutory and non-statutory providers. According to the white paper Caring for People, 'promoting choice and independence underlie all the Government's proposals', and the changes are intended to 'give people a greater individual say in how they live their lives and the services they need to help them do so' (1).

The 1992/3 East Sussex Community Care Plan, to which all the major statutory agencies locally have signed up (East Sussex County Council Social Services Department, East Sussex Family Health Services Authority, Brighton Health Authority, Eastbourne Health Authority and Hastings Health Authority), expands on this commitment. It argues that 'the services people receive and the way in which they are delivered are the result of a collection of values – broadly held beliefs about the rights of individuals and how they should be treated' (2). The values implicit in the Community Care Plan are then set out as follows:

- All individuals, no matter how disadvantaged or disabled, should have the greatest possible control over their lives.

- People should be able to live as independently as possible and to make informed decisions about their own lifestyle, including taking risks if they choose to do so.

- People should have access to up-to-date information about community care services.

- People have a right to express their wishes and priorities and to be personally involved when plans are made for their care.

Users first

- People should be treated with respect.

- People using community care services have a right to privacy and to be treated with dignity.

- People have a right to expect that their contact with, or any information they give to, the statutory agencies will be treated confidentially.

It is within the context of these national and local developments that the Department of Community Studies at the University of Brighton presented a one day conference entitled 'Users First, the REAL Challenge for Community Care' at the University's Conference Centre in Eastbourne in June 1992. While the ostensible commitment to user led services both nationally and locally is not in doubt, the organisers were aware that there are numerous theoretical and practical problems to be faced. What does 'user led' really mean? Participation comes in many guises. People can be informed, involved or take control. How does an increased role for users impinge on that of professionals? Does the empowerment of users disempower service providers, or can an effective partnership be built between the two? How can individual choice be enhanced in a climate of severe resource constraint?

The conceptual framework – users as consumers?

The notion of consumerism which underlies much of the policy concerning user involvement has been critically examined and found wanting in a public service context.(3) While it does assert that users have a right to be heard and consulted about aspects of service delivery, which can be a welcome antidote to excessive paternal benevolence by professionals, it is inherently limited in scope. The commercial analogy implies that users choose between available products and that as more people purchase popular brands production will increase to meet demand. This cannot happen in a cash limited public service. Despite the notion of consumer sovereignty, it is also debatable whose interests are really being served by any commercial enterprise. Products are marketed to consumers, and consumer satisfaction is ultimately of importance as a means to the end of company profits.

In the public sector the product itself is of a different order of magnitude. Health and welfare services are public services because of their fundamental importance to the quality of users lives – sometimes literally a matter of life and death. Service users are themselves involved in the process of production, ie the patients/clients have things done to them, they are the raw material, the ingredients.(4) There is therefore a presumptive need for a greater involvement in the processes of service planning and delivery as well as in the assessment of service outcomes than is usually accorded to consumers.

At the same time, many users are very vulnerable by virtue of the needs that have made them service users, and lacking in technical know how. Effective involvement will need support. It is clear how 'Users First' came to be defined as the REAL challenge for Community Care!

The objectives of this conference were to explore some of these underlying issues through key note speakers, but also to translate the answers into a practical context, of just how to put users first in a variety of service contexts, to consider for example, potential strategies and structures for enabling elderly people or mental health users to take a lead in the development of their own community care services locally. The emphasis on practice would hopefully provide a context for lesson learning

The process of user involvement

There are already examples available of how **not** to involve users. The Greater London Association of Community Health Councils (GLACHC) in a recent review of user involvement in the NHS outlines four models to be avoided. Although acknowledged as caricatures, they do encapsulate some of the major pitfalls.(5)

The first model is referred to as the **'Tell me you love me'** approach. This is concerned with assessing patient satisfaction with current services, frequently using patient surveys which often produce very high levels of satisfaction. The main weaknesses here are that the agenda addressed is defined by professionals rather than patients and is often confined to hotel issues rather than treatment outcomes. It is not always clear what satisfaction means, possibly gratitude and relief at being served per se as much as satisfaction with the quality of the service.

Model Two, or the **'Kill them with kindness'** approach, endeavours to compensate for past neglect by overwhelming individual users and/or users groups with participation opportunities. There is, however, little attention given to the processes of enabling effective participation to take place, ie the provision of relevant information, the use of jargon free language and suitable meeting times.

The **'Godfather'** approach on the other hand, attempts to identify one clearly defined spokesperson for each user category, who will be expected to represent their views in all contexts, inappropriately assuming a consensus of interests and views which is inherently stigmatising and discriminatory.

Finally GLACHC castigates the **'Puppet show'** approach, whereby the provider organisation attempts to by-pass existing established user groups by setting up their own ad hoc body. These may well cover a broad spread of membership but participants often do not have roots in the relevant communities and as terms of reference and agendas are invariably set by the providing body which has created them their independence is compromised.

The conference proceedings

The organisers of this conference were aware that elements of all four models are in widespread existence, but were also convinced that examples of good practice had developed and could and should be shared. Workshops focusing on client groups and led by people currently involved in such initiatives were thus a key component of the study day. These workshops, supported by input from the keynote speakers, were briefed to discuss how to achieve effective user involvement. Although, as the reports demonstrate, each addressed its brief rather differently according to the composition of the group – indeed the morning and afternoon sessions of the same groups were very different – they all identified key issues and made suggestions how these challenges might be satisfactorily resolved, drawing on their experience of existing projects in South East England. Considerable effort was made by the conference organisers to ensure that users themselves attended. Reduced rates were offered, and the policy was so successful that users were the majority in some discussion groups and able to set the agenda.

That the discussion groups were able to function so well is thanks to the helpful stimulation provided by the three speakers, Alison Wertheimer, Marion Beeforth and Pat Donlan, who spoke from the three complementary perspectives of policy analyst, service user and service provider respectively. From their papers it is clear that many of the challenges for service providers to which they drew attention were taken on board by the workshop groups. The need to define clearly what everyone understands by participation, emphasised by Alison Wertheimer, was an obvious starting point. The Learning Disability Group and the Mental Health Users Group both reported discussion on strategies for moving to a more participatory involvement from an information/consultation format and the implications for management of sharing control. The Physical Disability Group also discussed user management of budgets. This led to debates about the nature of a potential partnership between users and providers, a topic which had been introduced by Pat Donlan in his paper. The AIDS group were concerned that the effective empowerment of users might disable providers, although the Learning Disability Group argued that one was impossible without the other ie that 'that there was no way users could become empowered if the professional staff involved felt they were disempowered themselves'.

The costs of user involvement, graphically illustrated by Marion Beeforth, obviously struck a chord, as it was an issue picked up by several groups. These costs are not only the financial ones of meeting the expenses of attending meetings, but also the emotional ones of 'coming out' as a user of mental health or AIDS related services. All too often service providers assume that because users want to participate the opportunity to do so is a free gift. Hopefully this lesson at least has been learnt by those providers who attended the conference.

Users training needs, and the importance of relevant information if participation is to be effective, were associated issues discussed by the Learning Disability and Physical Disability Groups, but even if these needs are met, it was suggested that some users will find it hard to speak for themselves. The theme of advocacy appears prominently in the reports of several group discussions, particularly in that for older people, which also incorporated promising examples of current advocacy schemes. How to avoid user participation becoming an elitist exercise potentially conferring service advantages on the participants was an issue raised by the AIDS group, who proceeded to suggest a range of informal recruitment techniques.

In the light of the Government's frequent emphasis on the family basis of community care – 'The greater part of care has been, is and always will be provided by families and friends' (6) – it is important to note Alison Wertheimer's distinction between the needs of users and secondary users or carers. Both the Mental Health Users and Learning Disabilities workshops emphasised that users did not always feel that their family's perceptions of their needs necessarily reflected their own. Mental health users insisted on their need for speedy access to professional help.

These are only some of the issues discussed in the papers which follow. Much of the detailed debate that took place has inevitably been lost in the transcription, but hopefully what has been captured gives a flavour of the proceedings and constitutes a valid record of the main points made. This publication is very much a working document. Some of the questions raised remain unanswered, some of the conflicts noted unresolved, but hopefully others may be interested in sharing in these deliberations and will find some of the suggestions made helpful.

Over 80 people attended this conference and these reports demonstrate that despite the many practical difficulties there are both providers and users with a strong commitment to putting users first. Some promising initiatives are already in place, and if this day's proceedings encourage all those involved to continue to meet the challenge and enthuse a few others to set out on the road, it will be a fitting memorial to Brian Hamilton Cramp for whom 'empowering peoples lives' was a central concern.

References

1   Cm 849 Caring for People, Community Care in the Next Decade and Beyond HMSO London 1989

2   Caring for People in East Sussex, Community Care Plan 1992/3 Vol 1 1992

3   Potter J – Consumerism and the public sector, how well does the coat fit? Public Administration 1988 pp. 148–64

4   Stacey M – The health service consumer, a sociological misconception, Sociological Review Monograph 22 University of Keele 1976

5   Levenson R and Joule N – Listening to People, User involvement In the National Health Service, the challenge for the future, Greater London Association of CHCs , London 1992

6   Caring for People op cit.

Conference
Papers

2 User participation in community care: the challenge for services

Alison Wertheimer
Policy Analyst Kings Fund

My own 'stake' in this issue of participation is as an interested 'outsider' 'observer' and possible future user. I have recent experience with the National Health Service Training Executive and the Kings Fund which has involved the production of written materials for managers in the NHS, Social Service Departments and voluntary organisations, the identification of elements of 'good' practice – what works as well as what doesn't work- and the gathering for users, carers and managers of material on different local initiatives.

Why has user participation become flavour of the month?

Users have been going on about it for years, but people in the services are behaving as though it were a new discovery. The White Papers, Caring for People and Working for Patients, and subsequent legislation linked to changes in community care, emphasise consumer choice, and the development of services responsive to individuals' needs and wishes. 'Give people a much better opportunity to secure the services they need', 'stimulate public agencies to tailor services to individuals' needs', 'promote choice as well as independence', are fine sounding words. But what is the substance?

At an individual level separation of purchasing and providing **should** enable users to have a say about what sort of services are purchased on their behalf. At a wider level the legal requirement for planners to consult with users and carers **should** provide increased opportunities for users to influence the shape of future services. In theory, at least, a mixed economy of care should, the Government maintains, enable users to exercise some choices about how their needs are met by services. I am sceptical about all this, because health and social services seem to have barely begun to address some of the issues involved if user participation is really to mean anything other than a sentence in the mission statement or business plan or whatever.

What are some of these issues as identified by the users and carers? By the term 'users' I am referring to people who directly use community care services – people with learning difficulties, people with mental health difficulties, elderly people, people with physical or sensory disabilities, people with AIDS or who are HIV+ and so on. Informal and unpaid carers I would describe as secondary users – unless we are referring to services whose primary aim is to meet the needs of carers. It is important to make this clear. Much of my work is around people with learning difficulties – where other family members are still often the ones who are consulted.

What do we mean by participation?

There are a lot of words floating around: participation, consultation, consumerism, user control, involvement, choice. We need to try and ensure that service users and service workers are using the same language, and that they mean the same thing when they use the same word. Take the example of multi-disciplinary working. For one person with a physical handicap, it meant eight different professionals, 'who come in, drink my coffee, finish the milk, don't replace it, and leave me with the washing up'. I doubt whether the professionals saw it that way. For a young woman with learning difficulties, participation is being able to say what a good life is. Participation concerns peoples lives, and not just the services they use. We need to ask, 'are people empowered in their lives?' and not focus only on the services being offered.

The idea of a continuum is helpful. It can range from information: e.g. telling you what is being done, through consultation e.g. asking you what you want rather than having already decided what you're going to do, through partnership e.g. trying to decide together what should be done, and finally to delegated control e.g. letting you get on and do it!

Ways of 'doing' user participation

Until recently, consultation was probably the most common format. It reflects the way services work, holding one-off conferences or meetings, sending out a small mountain of papers, little speeches, polite questions, thank-you for coming. How congenial to users are the formal structures involved? They tend to attract users who feel comfortable with that way of doing things – white, middle class, articulate (like me!). It is not surprising if others vote with their feet. Professionals then label them apathetic, not interested, and users get the blame.

There are many other forms of participation, less formal meetings, smaller groups, opportunities for one to one, user forums and user groups, formal and informal survey work which includes qualitative and not just quantitative aspects, user-led evaluation, user involvement in staff training, collective and individual self-advocacy, user representatives on planning groups, on purchasing committees – the list is endless. Why not ask users how they want to be involved? There is more chance of getting it right if you ask people first. This will demonstrate your commitment to user empowerment, but you need to allow time for this. Users may need time and information in order to explore the options.

Can formal structures be made more user-friendly with people participating, not just observing? Do people need to be there for the whole meeting or just their bit? Are there tapes for people who are unable to read ? If surveys are the name of the game do you really need a structured questionnaire or can you build in opportunities for people to talk freely about their concerns?

Be prepared to experiment; don't worry if you get it wrong. Mistakes will be made if you are adventurous and experimental. Shared learning between workers and users might even bring you closer together!

Not so much a project – more a way of life

User participation is not something to tack on to reorganisation, budgeting and planning. It is easy to forget that user involvement, user choice, user control are, or should be, at the heart of the changes taking place. There is a danger of hiving it off as a discrete activity, something done by just one or two workers – often those workers given little power within the organisation. They are effectively marginalised, with uncertain resourcing. There is a lack of long term planning.

Participation must be built into everything the organisation does – policy-making, planning, budgeting, personnel, service delivery, management, monitoring and evaluation. It must be owned by everyone and on everyone's agenda and seen as everyone's responsibility, not delegated to a few.

Users first

Participation is not about 'one-offs', an annual users and carers conference, an annual consultation on the community care plan, an annual get together for local users and the Director of the Social Service Department. It is not a static but a continuing activity.

Commitment to participation needs to be sustained over time. Professionals have a habit of changing jobs often but users don't. They are, in most cases, always going to be users. What may seem like a project to a service worker is someone else's life.

Participation is personal

Human services tend to preach distance between staff and users with 'it's professional' as an excuse. We do 'get to know you' exercises with users. What about the other way round? I've had a lot of feedback that users appreciate time getting to know managers. This is best done at informal times, not in meetings but at lunches before or after meetings. Getting to know each other can help us understand what each other's stake in services is.

Many senior managers are remote from users and thence from the reality of users' experiences which may even be rationalised as 'soft data' or 'you can't generalise from one person's experience', thus invalidating a person's lived experience at a stroke! Maybe it's a defence against hearing about other people's pain. Humankind cannot bear too much reality.

Having regular personal contact with users may make for more honest relationships, even more equal relationships. Users don't want to be patronised, they want honesty and straightforwardness, even if that means being told that there are real constraints to developing new services. You don't stop being a manager just because you get involved in participation. It remains to ask how we get there, by what combination of carrots and sticks. I have doubts about building user participation into individual performance reviews of managers, but it is a possibility.

Leadership

It may sound strange when we're talking about more bottom up and less top-down approaches to service planning and delivery, but strong leadership and commitment to user participation by top managers, the people with power, is crucial.

There are a lot of messages coming through that senior managers will turn to user participation when everything else is sorted out, but this is too late. It is necessary to build it in now, to involve users in purchasing arrangements, contracts for providers, complaints systems, and quality assurance. We need senior managers who 'walk not talk the job', who don't only go into services at Christmas time for the glass of sherry and a mince pie.

It is important that leadership supports staff at all levels, including those on the front lines. Staff need that support. User participation is not cosy. It will often involve being challenged and criticised. Brickbats from users, often justifiable, need to be complemented by support from their managers. This will help staff to be open and not discouraged and defensive.

Support means allocating resources. User participation can't be a deferred budget item. It also means recognising that staff need to spend time with users to develop a working partnership with them. How many staff in community care are able to spend time with users other than in doing what has to be done? It also means senior managers being willing to act on what is fed back from staff in direct contact with service users. Front-line staff and users need to be clear how what they have to say will be dealt with.

Power

This always sounds like a bit of an old chestnut. It is mentioned ritualistically before we move swiftly on to something else, something easier. We could perhaps rationalise this evasion by claiming that the power of people who run services is hard to define, but power is something you recognise when you haven't got it. I suspect most users have a very vivid sense of what it is like to lack power.

I suggest that it's something which people working in services tend not even to think much about, unless, perhaps they are involved with compulsory admissions to mental hospital or child care orders. But make no mistake, it's there. Its existence is demonstrated when people feel it's unsafe to criticise services because they might lose the support they get, however unsatisfactory that is. Power is inherent in the fact that services often do things to or for people, not with them? Maybe this is something individual staff need to address for themselves? Where and in what ways do I exercise power over people?

It is easy to retreat into defensiveness – 'we've always done things that way and these are our procedures' – so, by implication, don't challenge us. In itself, this is a manifestation of power. Beware the slogans which compare community care to shopping at the local market.

Resources for participation

If it will cost at a personal level, it will also cost financially if it is going to progress beyond tokenism. User participation requires human and financial resources. Providing these gives clear messages that the services mean business. Properly run events cost money, staff time, sitter costs, transport costs, interpreters, refreshments. Other support can be in the form of free mail shots, photocopying, access to phones.

But, and this is often where things begin to stick, what about resourcing users and handing over control of those resources, not just phones and your franking machine, but enabling users to have their own phones? Some of the most effective user groups have been those with their own budgets, enabling users to hire their own workers. You might even consider, although it is virtually unheard of in statutory bodies, paying your own users for the work they do. Are users inevitably unpaid volunteers ? Newcastle Mental Health Users Group pays user representatives. It is interesting how District Health Authorities and Local Authorities will shell out thousands of pounds for 'consultants' but reckon to consult users free of charge!

Who sets the agendas?

Agendas are referred to here in their widest sense. Aro we seeking 'user managed participation or managed user participation'? Are we concerned not just with what gets talked about but with the whole how, when and where of user participation?

We also need to ask who decides on the form of participation. If an organisation needs information do they check out whether users think it's the right sort of information and whether it will be gathered in a user-friendly way – or do researchers plunge in and set up their 'research on users' willy nilly?

Who decides on time scales? These are a frequent source of complaints from users, when they are given a week to digest and comment on a bulky document. Even user activists have a life outside being an activist. Do users have to fit into an authority planning cycle, or are there ways in which cycles can be made flexible enough to adapt to users? Meetings which are always convened by service providing agencies mean that agencies control the agendas. How about agencies going out and meeting people on their own territories where it is users who set the agenda?

Having clear aims and outcomes

This issue needs to be addressed at different levels, but it is possible to have an overarching strategy, giving a clear understanding of WHY user participation is supported, what outcomes are desired, and how these will be measured. How will everyone know whether a particular initiative is working or not?

Users themselves need to be clear what their expectations are. What are they being asked to participate in? What will happen as a result?

For example, if users' view are being sought,

* Why is this being done?

* How will that information be used?

* What changes will result for users – how will their lives be affected?

It is important to be clear about whether you are consulting, asking people to work in partnership or what you are doing. Be honest about this. If you're not, the result will be cynicism, frustration and apathy. Users need to see some very clear measurable changes early on which will help sustain commitment. Users are easily frustrated by the time scales of bureaucracies.

Everyone needs to be clear about who is responsible for what. We've all been at meetings where someone has a complaint about a service and is told 'not our business, sorry'. This is bound to happen. Users don't live in a world of neat service boundaries and responsibilities, nor should they have to. But if you are planning a meeting, decide beforehand how these queries are going to be dealt with.

Tokenism

To recap, participation isn't something you do on every third Wednesday in a month with an 'A' in it, or once a year, or something which is delegated to one fairly junior member of staff. That is 'active tokenism', unfocussed thinking which fails to take on board the real meaning of participation.

Tokenism creeps in in various guises:

- Involving users too late: e.g. you've already decided what to do.

- Setting limits on the sort of changes made in response to users' demands: e.g. you can have tea with or without sugar – you can even put the sugar in yourself (though we'll probably limit the number of spoonfuls) – but we won't consider starting an employment service even if you say you'd rather have jobs than come to the day centre.

- Of course you can take part in our meetings: but we choose when the meetings take place, and where, and on what day of the week; and we decide how the meetings are run, and of course we set the agenda. Then some time later comes the comment, 'Pity the users don't seem interested in taking part'.

- Thinking too small: what about users on Trust boards? What about more users in local authorities as members or senior officers?

Summing up: key messages for people working in services

- Be clear what you mean by participation and see that everyone, including users, shares the same definition.

- Be clear about your aims and your outcomes. If you don't know where you want to go you won't be able to decide how to get there.

- Remember there are many different ways of involving users. Limiting your strategies will limit the number of users who get involved.

- Participation is not a project – it's a way of life. It's for everyday, not just once or twice a year or when you remember to do it.

- Participation is personal – you might even get to like it.

- Effective participation needs strong and committed leadership.

- Real participation means recognising where the power lies and acting on that knowledge.

- Participation needs proper resources – it doesn't come free.

- And finally a health warning: participation could seriously endanger your sense of complacency – but it almost certainly will not damage your health.

3 Users are people

Marion Beeforth
Chair of Brighton Insight

Introduction

I am currently a user of mental health services and have been for more years than I like to remember. I have spent many years in various psychiatric hospitals at one time for more than a decade as a revolving door patient, which means that I spent most of the time as an in-patient coming out from time to time, quite unable to cope with life outside, and then going back into hospital. I've had lots of ECT, and have found myself in a locked ward more than once. Considering all things I've always been treated reasonably well. Nevertheless I have experienced some weird and strange experiences.

During the 1980s mental health service users started to come together in order to speak out about how they had been treated and to lobby for user input to both the delivery and planning of services. Early user groups included the Patients' Councils in Nottingham, the Milton Keynes Advocacy Group and the Brighton INSIGHT group. 'Survivors Speak Out' was an early national organisation of individual users; MINDLINK's user members give a user input to National MIND; and we have formed UKAN (United Kingdom Advocacy Network) which is a network of user groups. The national organisations have each evolved their own character and they aim to complement each other rather than duplicating work.

The case for consulting service users

It is important to note at the outset that mental health services are set up to be a **service** for those who have mental health problems. Let us consider some other services and see whether mental health services should rightly include the word 'service' in their title.

- If for example you were going to have repairs done to your car and took it to the garage would you expect to be consulted? would you expect to give permission?

- How about when you use an Estate Agent – do you want to have feedback? Do you expect them to be on your side?

- When you go on holiday – do you expect to decide where you go, where you stay and what you have to eat?

- If you move to a new area – do you want to choose where you live and with whom you live ?

- If you went to the dentist would you expect to be able to say when it hurt? Would you expect to choose which dentist to go to and not to have to see someone who had hurt you last time ? Would you want to choose whether to have an injection or not?

Traditionally, mental health service users' feelings have been ignored because of their 'mental state'. They are treated as second class citizens. Most people experience emotional distress. It is part of life's rich panoply of experience from which no one is immune. No one expects it to happen to them, but it does! When it does the services are meant to benefit users, but it doesn't always feel like that!

We'd like mental health workers to remember that they wouldn't have any jobs if there were no users. As users we experience too much of workers playing for 'political' points. We really can do without all the hassle of professional non-cooperation. Often it feels as though users really are the experts, because we have to find out for ourselves what is available, who is who and who does what. People will be much more likely to use services and to be cooperative if they are 'user friendly'.

Professional attitudes to service users

Service workers do not always treat users with respect as people.

There are a range of situations where this is so. For example:

- Receptionists assume they are always right. Why do they always believe that we are the ones who make mistakes?

- Confidentiality and privacy are denied us. Should not lockers for personal possessions be able to be locked ?

- Why can't we talk privately with those who help us?

One particular area where professionals often display insensitive behaviour concerns appointments. Professionals can cancel appointments at short notice. Appointment times may be inconvenient for us and yet we have to feel grateful. We are not allowed to be late. Workers usually do not have to battle with trains and buses, they have their offices on site, but we users are often kept waiting for long periods with no explanations. Emergencies can always occur but we should not be kept waiting for spurious reason. It is important that respect is paid to people. We would like workers to manage their diaries properly!

Workers can cancel appointments at short notice because they have 'just remembered' a meeting. It would be much appreciated if they were honest enough to say 'I forgot'.

We may have a job. Even the most unlikely people may eventually find a job. We can get time off for an appointment, but cannot take unlimited time off, and we may lose pay if we do so. Workers need to be aware of how important these jobs are to us. It is difficult to get a job if you are a user. Therefore it is important to us that we keep our jobs. Time off is not easy to arrange when you're trying to prove yourself, and the jobs available to us are likely to be lowly ones. Workers should be conscious of what it is they are expecting their client to do, and what that entails for the client.

Everyone is a valued person. We should be involved in decisions affecting our lives, especially those involving risk. Such risks might be the side effects of medications, not knowing what these might be. We are often left to worry about it, thinking we are getting worse. I will co-operate with treatment willingly if I have the right information.

Quality of life in the community

Life in the community can be very, very hard. Often we users are institutionalised because we have used the service. We have become accustomed to:

- other people knowing what's best for us, so we are thought to be submissive;

- other people telling us what to do which leads to a lack of initiative;

- learning that people never listen to what we want, which leads to apathy;

- having no real choices which causes us to be indecisive.

All of these attributes are said to be symptoms of our so called mental illnesses. We have to learn to obey unwritten rules in order to be thought to be better, but even in distress we can be aware of what is happening. So we are trying to survive in the community with all these problems.

Adjusting to life in the community

We have to acquire skills just to exist in the community. I'm not talking about such things as cooking or budgeting. Do workers know that there is a real world out there? It sometimes feels as though they all inhabit a different planet. There is a feeling of complete separateness. No-one outside wants to know what or how users really feel. We feel guilty, we feel apprehensive, we certainly feel inadequate, but our families expect us to be well because we are living in the community.

Because we have no physical problems there is no convalescent period, particularly if you are a woman. I'd like to have a plaster cast I could strap on to my arm at times of stress. Maybe then people would accept that I can't do anything more! Facing people is difficult, and there are the side- effects of drugs, panic attacks, tiredness and exhaustion. Once I actually believed I was a computer – with whom is it possible for me to share feelings like this?

The quality of life for users is of utmost importance. We need to feel good about ourselves, to feel safe and secure. We need somewhere to go and meet friends, and we would like a choice of places to go or a choice of activities to do during the day. We want to be mobile, to have money for bus fares, bus passes or whatever

We want to feel cared about not necessarily cared for. We would like to have opportunities for learning about new pastimes: new hobbies, swimming, languages, carpentry, dress making to name but a few.

We have to learn to realise when we need help. It should be easy to ask for help and that help should be readily available and we should not be abandoned during periods when we are well. We want to feel part of the community, but we would like workers to appreciate all that this involves.

Dealing with the general public

We are the ones who have to put up with public attitudes. We have to learn to deal with the public's hostility on every level from 'we'd be better locked up' to being ignored completely. To be treated as a full member of society is really quite a novelty for us. If mental health users were to treat us with respect and courtesy then others would be encouraged to do the same. The common courtesies of life which are so important to everyone are often denied us.

What does it mean to have user participation in planning?

As demonstrated below user participation in planning needs a change in the viewpoint of the professionals involved.

Figure 1

> ### The official's view
>
> - we're providers of mental health services
> - we know what is best
> - we have to organise services
> - we must have user participation
> - let's set up a users group
> - do we know any users we can ask?

Professionals need to be clear whether they actually want users to be involved, or whether they are already convinced that it will not work. User involvement in planning means asking users to come on to your planning committees. It is important that the users invited are selected by users and are not people who the professionals feel would 'fit in' with the committee. Professionals should be prepared to accept the users' representative as equal members of the committee; be prepared to listen to the users' points of view. It may be difficult for professionals to do this and to take the representative seriously. There are a number of questions that can usefully be asked such as:

- Are users informed when and if a meeting is cancelled?

Users first

- Are they given an opportunity to speak?

- Are you prepared to offer them a lift in your car?

- What about mental health jargon?

Participation is stressful for users, and it is important to bear in mind that they often feel more comfortable in pairs. There are also other practical difficulties to be overcome. How do you avoid 'tokenism' – the idea that because we have two users on our committee that is all right. They may be there, but who listen to the users? Who takes notice of what they say? Is it obvious to users that their efforts are not in vain?

A strong user group

If users are to take a real role in the planning process then users as a group have to identify the issues that they are most concerned about. It is also necessary for them to decide whether it is worth taking the risk of speaking out. It is important to stress that there can be a very real risk for users in speaking out. It can be easier (for them) when user representatives are members of a strong user group, because they will get support and strength from the group to do this daunting work.

How to set up a user group

I am often asked how professionals can set up a user group. But it really doesn't happen quite like that. My suggestions are summarised below.

Figure 2

How to involve users

- get users together

- leave us alone to talk

- invite us onto your committees

- listen to what we say

- give us information

- pay our expenses

These are the basic necessities for a new user group. However, it is important to remember that users are poor, they are usually on benefits, and they do not have access to typewriters, photocopiers, telephones or secretaries.

The Authorities can be disbelieving of the fact that users can speak up for themselves. This attitude can be very difficult to overcome, for doing so involves a new way of working for providers of services! It can be a learning process for both users and professionals. Users' actual experiences can be more valuable than professionals' theory and practice. However it is important to remember that users are people and they should have rights. Workers have their problems outside their working lives; users have problems which are not secret. In the planning process both these types of problems have to be set aside, but it may be particularly difficult for professionals to set aside their known perceptions of particular people.

The reality of user involvement

The Brighton Insight Group was established in 1987 to further the written commitment of the area's statutory services of involving users in the planning of mental health services. Members of Brighton Insight came together to share their experiences, to work together to try to change the way in which services are planned and delivered, to improve housing and job opportunities and also to try to remove the stigma given to mental health service users. Members of Brighton Insight have worked hard over the past five years to achieve their reputation, not only locally but also nationally. Our members now sit on planning and steering groups, they have given valuable input to a peer advocacy scheme, they helped to establish a Brighton Users' Charter (before such charters became politically fashionable) and they are asked regularly to give talks and to run training sessions. These achievements have been secured in spite of the fact that any episode of mental illness affects a person for the rest of his/her life and that mental health service users have to struggle to survive.

There are other user involvement issues which are not so well known. For instance there are workers who have furthered their careers and enhanced their reputations because they pioneered 'user participation'. However, this has often been achieved at the expense of the users themselves. It is true that the users' self-esteem grows and they become more confident, but have our efforts gained us rewards in the form of well paid employment and better housing? Are the public more aware of our problems? Are mental health services any better? I am often asked to contribute comments and to produce reports on mental health matters, but as I don't have a secretary it seems to me that I often work harder than those professionals I meet on committees. I use my own phone at home. Who pays the rental? I spend a lot of time travelling to meetings and I have a car. Who pays the garage bills? I have a scientific training and have my own computer. I am committed to 'user participation' and I do enjoy the work. But is it right that in effect I 'pay' to do this work? Even travel expenses are not always readily available, and users are poor.

The stress for users engaged in this work is considerable. The work is very demanding. If we did not have our mental health problems we would not be users. We are 'vulnerable', and yet we are often asked to do more than we feel able to. If we cannot cope this can then be cited as evidence of the impossibility, or rashness, of 'user' involvement.

Workers stay in one post for two or three years on average before they move on. I have lived in the same area for more than twenty years and have seen generations of workers come and go. New workers when they arrive all seem to want to start the process of 'user participation' from scratch (the new broom effect), regardless of the work that the local users have already achieved and the existence of groups struggling to survive without support. The Insight Group was fortunate to be given an office in our new Community Mental Health Centre. It was expected, or rather just assumed, that it would be staffed full time, but we had no paid worker. It was also expected that we would change the venue for our weekly meetings and we actually had to discover this fact for ourselves because no-one bothered to inform us. We are now expected to hold our weekly meetings in a building where workers have their offices. The room reserved for our meetings is not private, with the likelihood of people walking through during our meetings. The chairs are uncomfortable, and we are not permitted to make our own tea/coffee because the cafe downstairs 'had to make a profit'!

Requirement of user involvement

Letting a user group be independent means giving enough support to allow the group to function without dictating to that group what it should, or should not, do. It is important for me to point out that if a group is truly a user group then professionals should have no direct control over what happens after a group has been set up.

We feel strongly that we do have a point of view to put forward. Sympathetic workers have been more than generous to me in sharing some of their skills, and individual workers have given their time freely to help me. There are many opportunities for users to become involved, but not all do want to get involved. Some have skills they acquired before they had problems, but others have never had the opportunity to learn any such skills. Users need to have the resources to train and support those who want and need training. User groups do not properly fit into the same category as other voluntary organisations because they need to be resourced and supported in ways which have regard for users' particular needs.

For full 'user involvement' users should be consulted at all levels of decision making, not only in planning groups but in one to one therapeutic relationships and also in day and residential services. The range of potential opportunities is summarised below.

Figure 3

> ## Levels of user participation
>
> - one to one relationships (maybe therapeutic)
>
> - hospital, group home, day centre
>
> - district, area
>
> - county, regional
>
> - national
>
> - international

Involvement in the 'user participation' movement is not easy. The work is very demanding and we often find ourselves working alongside the same workers that we rely on to help us.

Can workers accept that some users may become workers and therefore also become colleagues; that some users may at some time actually make managerial decisions and that services may be user-run? This does not mean that the statutory services will then be able to dissociate themselves from providing resources and support for these services. Are managers of mental health services really prepared to share control with users? As I said before, mental health services are meant to benefit the user. It doesn't always feel that this aim is achieved.

4 Empowerment and quality in community care

Pat Donlan, Director of Social Care
South East Institute of Public Health

Empowerment is the business of community care. Agencies have brought themselves into existence not only to provide housing and local services outside the 'institution', but to enable those disadvantaged by illness or disability to live as normal a life as possible. Normal life is not just a matter of location, but more a matter of quality. Early attempts to provide community based living for patients often failed simply because they resembled out-posted mini-wards, reflecting the institutional culture. Normal life will be different for each of us, and we achieve it in differing degrees. It is essentially learning to deal with the intricacies of human social life and to experience personal achievements, successes, mistakes and failures. For the disadvantaged, it happens when those who have the power to control through their caring choose not to control.

People who require care are often disadvantaged because they are devalued by the systems of care surrounding them. These systems can fail to engage the service user in a positive human way simply because of the fierce demand on limited facilities and skills. However, the more dangerous depreciation of service users happens during the subtle manoeuvres of care which promote dependence.

Normal living is what we want for ourselves as carers. We must not allow our systems or our caring to frustrate those using our services in their struggle for a more normal life.

Community care must carry with it a primary focus on empowerment of the service user. Community care agencies promote empowered living by sharing information and planning together with service users and their carers. Recognising together the benefits of enhanced understanding and participation will help us all manage the uncomfortable moments of criticism and authentic negotiation between service users, commissioners, and providers. It is this joint activity in the service negotiating process that empowers. Negotiating for the optimal outcome within the constraints of resources uplifts users' determination to make their voice heard in a way that makes a difference. Together service users and providers work out a service which does not devalue or endanger dependence – something of quality!

Empowerment

Every human being develops some competence in empowered living from the very earliest months of life. Through the years most people respond to normal family or social influences which effectively identify acceptable and unacceptable use of personal power. Most commonly these restraints are concerned with the rights of others within the society.

People are sometimes thwarted in their development of personal power. The influences of family or society give them the message that they are of lesser value than others, that because of some disability or illness they require assistance and looking after.

They come to understand that somehow they are of little worth and cannot be taken seriously. When these damaging influences act from the earliest stages of life, and are consistently re-enforced by society's care systems, the people affected by them become disadvantaged and learn to accept being devalued as a life script. Special recovery work and persistence is required to turn these disadvantaged people onto the road where raised expectations lead to improved self determination.

Recovery work begins with an understanding of the four major characteristics of empowerment.

1 Understanding

The development of understanding the situation which devalues and disadvantages is the starting point. This will require the candid sharing of information and, in the case of community care service users, would be prompted by the introduction of user-held records. The important element here is the grasping of the possibility of opportunities for change. The unsatisfactory situation does not need to continue.

2 Identifying making a voice

Understanding that the current situation is not good enough usually does not end there, but is followed by a compulsion to identify what is required to correct or improve that situation. People begins to say: "I would like this," or, "I want that," or eventually, "Why can't I do that for myself?" For the care service user it will be important that they have the central role in planning their services with the purchasers of those services.

'Planning in partnership' is becoming a common goal for care agencies, and while this is impressive, the service users had better understand the nature of partnerships. Good partnerships are essentially unequal, with each member of the partnership bringing particular attributes which somehow complement the other partner's strengths and compensate for weaknesses. It is often said that it is the differences, and not the similarities, that make for successful partnerships. The purchaser holding the power to buy the services required needs to be balanced by the service user to negotiate the most effective assistance.

3 Criticising making the voice heard

This is something that many people find difficult to do well and openly and without anger. They often feel as exposed and vulnerable when criticising as when receiving criticism. But once an appropriate and realistic solution to the disadvantaging situation is identified, this has to be the next stage if no change occurs. This may require some learning of assertive communication techniques.

4 Negotiating making a difference

Negotiation is a skill that is uncommon amongst both service users and service providers. Initially the service user may be intent on securing the perceived ideal solution but, through the process of negotiation, will agree a more achievable response to their needs. The significant point here is that all parties must learn to negotiate effectively and positively, not allowing entrenchment to preclude the imaginative solution which leads to a mutually acceptable agreement.

Empowered living, then, is characterised by an enhanced ability to understand implications and subtleties, to discern priorities, to participate assertively, and to reach for true compromise rather than choosing from a shortlist of unsatisfactory options.

Measuring empowerment is measuring quality

If empowerment is the business of community care, measuring enhancements in empowered living also directly gauges the quality of the community care provision. Measuring enhancements really means understanding the level of empowerment at any starting point in time and identifying differences in that level at subsequent times. To ensure that those differences are a direct result of the community care services provided, it is essential that targeted achievements are agreed with the service user and are explicitly identified in the individual service plan. The services provided must then be designed to directly attain those targets.

Performance indicators are easily identified for each individual situation. They will become the benchmarks against which the success of community care provision can be judged. The five major areas of concern for measuring empowered living are listed here with possible performance indicators beneath them:

1 Degree of increased self-actualisation

- Number of competencies developed
- Types of competencies developed
- Increase in the number situations where the competencies are displayed

2 Degree of decreased non-disability associated dependency

- Degree of decrease in 'institutional' dependence
- Number of dependency-type behaviours diminished
- Types of dependency-type behaviours diminished

3 Degree of increased involvement in and quality of negotiation

- Change in the level of participation in planning
- Degree of persistence in presenting opinion
- Development of personal influence

4 Degree of increased expectations

- Shift in planning from care to independence

- Movement from the acceptable to the more acceptable

5 Degree that 'disadvantaged' people empower others

- Development of sense of responsibility toward community

- Development of opportunities for personal relationships

- Decrease in self-centred, reactive responses

- Opportunities to represent the views of others

Conclusion

Empowerment is the business of community care. The degree of excellence (quality) of community care services can be measured in direct relation to the degrees of empowerment achieved by the people using the services. The measurement of increased empowered living then becomes the most significant quality management tool. To know one is to know the other.

Workshop
Reports

5 Advocacy initiatives for older people

Group leader: Kat Pearce
Director of Age Concern, East Sussex
Reporter: Jackie Langley

It was apparent from discussion that advocacy initiatives for older people are still in their infancy and that the major issues are in the main the same as those for advocacy with any users. This report begins with the main points raised in discussion from the two sessions. This developed from the following questions: What is advocacy? Why do we need advocacy services? What are the problems of advocacy for users, staff and managers? The report concludes with information about two local initiatives and finally focuses on some of the challenges that advocacy with older people still has to meet.

What is advocacy?

A 'brainstorm' produced a long list of words and phrases which included: facilitating; to speak on behalf of/with/for; interpreting; enabling; empowering; championing; befriending; support; being independent; examining received wisdom – e.g. are there really no services available?

It also produced some thoughts about what advocacy isn't. These included: the misuse of power by putting forward your own views rather than those of the user; giving advice rather than information from which to make a choice/decision.

Advocacy refers to the process of articulating someone else's needs as they perceive them to secure services they require and/or rights to which they and their advocate believe them to be entitled.

It was acknowledged that the role of advocate can be a difficult one. It requires people to know where 'they are coming from' and to be able to suspend their own feelings and judgements about the user's situation and needs. An advocate needs to be able to listen, have some relevant knowledge, question service provision, accurately interpret the user's view of their world, their needs and wants and to be able to negotiate from the user's frame of reference.

It was argued that advocacy takes different forms and fulfils different functions. There are those advocates who work on a one-to-one basis with users which is known as Citizen advocacy. Self-advocacy is when someone acts on their own behalf to present their case in a fairly formal manner, or when a peer, e.g. another person with a disability, advocates on their behalf. Collective advocacy is where a group of people unite to campaign on issues affecting more than one individual. It was felt that another form of advocacy could be described as a community development approach – discovering what is needed in a community, to feed the information to service providers and in this way to obtain services wanted by those who need them.

Why do we need advocacy?

The group felt that users often need help to find their way through a maze of services.

Older people often find friends or relations speaking for them – most likely with their own agendas, perhaps as carers. In these circumstances the older person needs an advocate – a carer may need one of their own too.

Older people, it was argued, need advocates because they have a right to full lives, not just services – even so called 'needs led' assessments tend to be about a mix and match of services.

There are three actors in the provision of services to older people: the older person, care managers or staff in similar positions and those who actually provide the services. The power lioc with the latter two and an advocate can help redress the balance.

What are the problems of advocacy for users, staff and managers?

Is was felt that a professional worker can only act as an advocate for a user they are working with to a very limited extent. An example discussed was a worker from one agency acting as advocate for a user with another agency. Although this might achieve something for the user, the worker would need to maintain a working, negotiating, 'trade off' relationship with the other agency for the sake of future users and situations. This would inhibit the advocacy process.

It was agreed that an effective advocate must be independent. This raised questions, rather than provided answers, about how advocacy services are funded. Will social services or health department funding allow the service to be truly independent? 'They who pay the piper call the tune!'

Advocates for older people may find themselves representing the views of a user which could be seen as encouraging the continuation of a risky situation. Should they do this? Is the answer, for example, for a neighbour worried by the risk to have an advocate too?

Local advocacy projects

Information on two local advocacy projects was offered to the group as illustrations of the need for advocacy and how this might be met. Brighton Mind has a project concerning older people with mental health problems. As a group they are generally seen as incapable of making informed choices and the project aims to challenge this assumption firstly by giving people an opportunity to voice concerns about the services they receive, secondly by feeding issues of collective concern back to service management in an anonymous form and using Mind's organisational role to influence policy and procedure, and finally by encouraging services to respond to need and work towards needs led rather than service led provision.

The project works according to the principles of independence and confidentiality, adopting a non-judgmental approach, emphasising users' rights and stressing the importance of giving users information. To date concerns raised by users have included, a feeling that they are not believed by professionals, that they lack relevant information about treatment, their rights and the structure of services, that services are inflexible and that there is over hospitalisation because of lack of community support. There has however been positive feedback that staff are well intentioned , although also reports of rudeness and lack of compassion. Because of dependence on services, the project has encountered a fear of speaking out and some problems of communication in case reviews and ward rounds.

The second project referred to is run by Age Concern East Sussex to support older people in the care of Brighton Health Authority and East Sussex Social Services Department. This is being set up in response to a series of local policy initiatives which include the closure of a long stay hospital unit for frail older people and the introduction of a new complaints procedure by East Sussex Social Services Department. It will be managed by a joint advisory group and funded by Age Concern England and South Downs Health NHS Trust. This scheme is still at the planning stage but aims to recruit and train volunteer advocates, raise the awareness of care staff, identify and accumulate relevant information sources for users and help develop user involvement in the planning of services. It is intended that this project is evaluated and a report written so that lessons learned can be widely disseminated

Advocacy – challenges and questions for the future

The general conclusion of the group discussions was that advocacy is a difficult task. Advocates need training and support. Does this imply that advocacy will become a professional task? What is the future for the organisation of advocacy?

Advocacy needs to be independent, but does involve working with service providers. What should be the relationship between advocates and service providers? How can staff be helped to understand the nature of the role of advocate?

How do you convince an older person that the advocate is for her and not a representative of the service? How can he or she be supported if complaining from a vulnerable position e.g. in residential care?

How can you ensure that issues arising from one to one advocacy are fed into the service planning/service delivery systems? Befriending is a part of advocacy, but if it stops at that there may be a problem that the befriender fills the gap in service rather than taking it to a policy or planning level.

It could be argued that it is impossible to advocate on behalf of very disorientated or confused people. However evidence suggests that treated with respect, which sadly doesn't always happen, these users respond very differently and it may well be possible to discover their needs and wishes. Also in some circumstances the advocate can operate from a do 'as if' perspective. e.g. If you were asked to advocate for someone being moved from one long term care setting to another, you could work from an 'as if it were me' viewpoint. The question this raises is how do you know that the older person would feel the same?

Finally, older people generally have low expectations. Developing people's awareness of the possibility of, and a right to, a fuller life is a fundamental issue for those involved in advocacy for older service users.

6 Self help groups for people with HIV/AIDS

Group leader: A user from 'Our House BP' Brighton
Reporters: Bob Skelton and Sandra Winn

Origins of self-help groups for HIV/AIDS

The discussion group leader introduced the sessions by describing differences in the origins of self-help groups for people with HIV/AIDS in Brighton and New York. In the early days in New York, prior to the recognition of HIV as the cause of AIDS, self-help groups such as Gay Men's Health Crisis had originated as mutual support groups for gay men. Official agencies were not involved and empowerment was self-empowerment. Out of this necessity for self-help an articulate and confident group with high levels of self esteem emerged. The idea of safer sex was one outcome of this effort. Gay Men's Health Crisis has evolved into a large scale enterprise, supported by local government and involving many volunteers, and is now a long way from its origins in self-help groups.

As the virus spread, the population experiencing HIV/AIDS became less homogeneous and this is the case in both New York and Brighton today. In Brighton the population with HIV/AIDS is segmented and levels of self-esteem can be low. There is often a reluctance to engage in dialogue with service providers 'through the usual channels' and feelings of discontent with services do not necessarily lead to a large scale commitment to self-help.

Against this background Our House BP emerged. This is a self-help group in Brighton for those affected by HIV/AIDS, which came into existence in January 1991. Our House BP aims to meet a number of otherwise unmet needs, for example providing services for people in full-time work. It provides evening and weekend facilities including a Sunday drop-in with a lunch and other facilities such as massage, aromatherapy, money advice and emotional support. There are also evening support groups and a range of other groups and activities. After a previous failed attempt to set up a user group, Our House BP was the result of a response by users to the perceived frustrations with official agencies who were felt to be overlooking users' needs during a period of inter-professional debate about how best to establish a service.

Key issues facing self-help groups for HIV/AIDS

A number of issues were identified in the ensuing discussion. Firstly, the difficulties inherent in the dual role for users who are also active in self-help groups and who may therefore be in frequent dialogue with service providers were highlighted. In this role some power is achieved, of which a by-product may be a faster claim on services, which then has to be reconciled with the awareness that 'ordinary' service users may not be getting access to similar services.

Secondly, there is a need for self-help groups to act as advocates for service users. The issue for users is to represent their views to service providers in order to achieve the best service available from what is on offer. The users' perception is that services are often overly bureaucratic and slow to respond. To improve service delivery through advocacy may be a task which HIV/AIDS service users are uniquely placed to achieve, since their own self-help structures are relatively innovatory and flexible. In this respect Alison Wertheimer's comment in the opening session was noted. Service providers should be prepared to go where the users are and give them some lunch! Specifically, providers could help to train users for advocacy. This could be a valuable aid to the other essential process of raising self-esteem, itself a pre-requisite for the development of advocacy skills. Advocacy skills are essential since the impulse to the prompt delivery of services tends to come as a response to demands from users. It was noted incidentally that receptionists and similar gate-keeping staff might be less intimidating if they received HIV/AIDS awareness training.

Thirdly, the willingness and the capacity of users to engage in joint discussion with service providers was considered. It was pointed out that there is a small number of people locally who are frequently called upon to represent the views of users of HIV/AIDS services. At this particular conference, the HIV/AIDS discussion group was one of only two groups in which there was no user representation other than the group leader. It is sometimes suggested that users may not be concerned to get involved in discussion with providers because they are satisfied with the service provided. More likely, it was asserted, is that participation does not take place because there is a feeling on the part of users that they either do not understand what the structures have to do with their lives or the structures appear irrelevant to them. This is especially important for people with HIV/AIDS since the evidence seems to indicate that long term survivors are often those who get involved with self-help groups, challenge professionals, and are active.

Level of participation in self-help groups

The discussion then focussed on the level of participation in drop-in facilities. It was noted that facilities such as meals or other social events provide a helpful first point of contact with self-help groups. This may then lead on to a willingness to debate with service providers. When providers went to where the users were, and made lunch available, then users found they had something to say.

Participation in self-help groups depends not just on what is offered, but on what people perceive to be offered. This is significant in relation to the low level of participation of positive women in Our House BP. Thus self-help groups cannot simply adopt a pro-active 'ahead of the game' philosophy of designing structures which assume there will be a variety of groups who wish to be involved, because the expressed need may not be there. A number of reasons why women tended not to get involved were identified: groups such as Our House BP are seen by women as gay men's groups so that women may feel that the agenda will be dominated by gay men's issues; it is difficult, especially for women with children, to face the stigma of going to meetings; confidentiality in relation to HIV/AIDS makes it difficult to circulate invitations to meetings (networking may be the answer here for those women who would wish to join a group); women are less likely to want to join a group because they are schooled not to put their own needs first, so it may be important for women to feel they can make an active contribution to the group and contribute to the welfare of others.

Many of those who use Our House BP have experienced a sense of empowerment. Some people using the service are disabled and not working while others tend to be employed in social services, nursing and similar occupations in which it is easier to be open about their status than in many other occupations. Most empowering for users is the Our House positive speakers bureau, participation which can lead on to people wishing to do work in other areas, including campaigning. Experience has shown the importance of fitting the speaker to the audience wherever possible, so that identification can be experienced.

Quality of service provision

There has been a perception that service provision is good in Brighton compared with the rest of the UK (and the USA). This is because Brighton used the time lag between the general awareness of the impending epidemic and the onset of cases to good effect in terms of the preparation of services. There is a sense that this advantage has been lost in the past three years, although this perception may be the result of the increased empowerment of users, whereby people are becoming more impatient and more demanding of services.

It is important in relation to the provision of services for people with HIV/AIDS that delivery should be speedy and responsive to the changing needs of users. An example of the advantages of flexible services was provided by Gay Men's Health Crisis in the early days, when a volunteer system operated, in which volunteers were divided into buddies (who undertook practical and domestic tasks) and crisis intervention workers (counsellors). The distinction between these roles broke down in practice, but at the time Gay Men's Health Crisis was a sufficiently flexible organisation to deal with this by designating both types of volunteers as 'crisis management partners', trained to do both types of job. In general, though, organisations are perceived to be inflexible and to work on different time-scales to users. While this is a source of frustration, it was recognised that services for people with HIV/AIDS are not the worst offenders in this respect, because they are not encumbered with a long history of provision which has become ossified.

It was recognised that in comparison with HIV/AIDS services, users of other services can feel underprivileged. The point however was made strongly that the response to this should be to scale other services up, not to scale HIV/AIDS services down.

Service providers must recognise that if they genuinely want to involve service users in decisions about service delivery, then their stance has to go beyond the current rhetoric of mere assertion that 'users are part of the service'. Practical inducements to involvement have to be made, including, for example, the payment of fees and expenses.

Problems inhibiting service improvement

The afternoon session devoted a considerable amount of time to a discussion of the ability of service workers to provide an appropriate and effective service to users. Amongst the points considered were:

1   The problems that organisations may have in overcoming bureaucratic blocks in order to meet need on the part of users.

2   The perceived lack of training amongst workers which may prevent them confronting without fear and prejudice questions of sexuality, drug use and unconventional life styles.

3   That there may exist in principle a contradiction between empowering people and providing services. Will Social Service Departments be able to contemplate including users in decision making about the allocation of budgets for example? If empowerment involves thinking jointly about strategies to change the enterprise, will middle managers of services be able to contemplate alliances with users in relation to demands about the allocation of resources? Effective empowerment strategies will de-skill professionals and lead to challenges by service providers to managers. Such a state of affairs will generate problems for organisations in terms of their ability to deliver services.

4   Radical alliances of service providers and users may be difficult to create, because of fears on the part of users that public campaigns may expose them to stigmatisation and assault.

5   Rank and file workers themselves may feel disempowered and are therefore not necessarily the most effective allies for users. An associated difficulty is the tension often experienced by workers in relation to who they represent – themselves or their agency. This tension may make empathetic understanding of the user difficult and thus limit their capacity for effective representation of the user voice. Perhaps a way to begin to resolve this tension, it was pointed out, is to recognise that we are all users, in need of empowerment.

6   Finally, it was pointed out that activists in self-help groups are often doubly frustrated when on the one hand users or potential service users complain that there are no effective services, but do not want to do anything themselves to attempt to change the situation, while on the other hand the activist recognises that probably they are right and that not much can be done to improve the situation. In these circumstances perhaps the best that can be said is that that act of complaining itself has some therapeutic value!

Summarising

The key issues emerging from the discussion group can be identified as these: firstly, that the users' voice is critical. Their perspective is unique and must be taken into account when services for people with HIV/AIDS are being delivered. Secondly, that the task for providers in identifying the voice of those who use services for people with HIV/AIDS is a complex one. The felt stigma of some people with these conditions means that the users' voice is sometimes muted. This at the moment seems to be particularly the case, for example, in relation to HIV positive women, who are not well represented in self help groups, and is also the case for some men who, although they may be willing to make use of the physical and socio-emotional support offered by Our House BP, have not yet been convinced of the value of expressing demands to service providers. This relates to the third issue, which is that of the potential of relationships and strategies within the support group itself for developing self confidence and a sense of empowerment amongst participants. The final issue is a point to be made to service workers and service providers. What practical support, organisationally and financially, are you prepared to make available to assist processes of 'empowerment' for service users in order that this currently fashionable notion goes beyond mere rhetoric?

7 Involving people with learning difficulties

Group leader: Jill Winstone, Staff Development Officer
East Sussex Social Services Department
Reporter: Pat Charlton

Although users and service providers participated in the morning group, the afternoon group involved service providers only, but for the purposes of this account the content of both group discussions have been integrated.

Current local development – user participation

After introductions, participants agreed that they would be interested initially to hear from Jill Winstone about the current developments in user participation and involvement in the Brighton area of East Sussex Social Services.

It was explained that this had started with a working group made up of staff from day centres asking themselves basic questions about what was really meant by user involvement. Was it about increased consultation, or was it about reaching a stage where users had control of services in terms of budgeting, planning and staff selection? How much involvement might be needed, indeed wanted, by users? And on the provider side, was consultation on services enough? Recognition was given to the tension and possible conflict between agency needs and resources and users' individual, personal needs.

A realistic acknowledgement of the very limited and limiting experiences and lack of opportunities of service users to develop a 'collective voice', or perhaps a voice at all, or to make choices, had led to an initial plan starting 'where people were'. This involved seeking information from users to improve the efficiency and effectiveness of current services, and providing a means of feeding this information and viewpoints into the system. It also involved informing users and involving them as much as possible in changes and new developments, with the intention that ultimately users would be involved in the planning process of any new developments.

Users first

This framework for practice in both day and residential services supports user involvement on a day to day basis in a number of ways. This is through personal programmes to meet individual needs where service deficiencies can be picked up. Also through a Meet and Speak self advocacy group attended by people who use a variety of services over a wider area than just Brighton. This group is focussed on personal development, but it might also result in the group deciding to take up service issues with service providers. Additionally, user groups have been developed in day centres, and staff in residential centres have started addressing ways in which they can facilitate and support users in running their own groups.

At these groups, users will be supported and helped to develop, for example, understanding of the nature of meetings, and to participate with confidence, stress being placed on the need to start where people are now, and to develop at their own pace, thus avoiding tokenism and further loss of power and control.

Planned developments will involve user representatives from each day centre becoming members of a Brighton Day Services Group, and in turn members of this group will be elected to sit on a panel which will include staff, parents and carers also. While recognising the need for training and development for both service users and facilitators, and the positive encouragement of service users to participate, it was accepted that involvement must be at the users choice. Finally, underlying all these initiatives were the 'Five Service Accomplishments' (John O'Brien), or basic essentials; choice, dignity and respect, the development of new skills and competencies, opportunities to make relationships, and community involvement.

These very interesting and encouraging developments stimulated questions on specific details, and further discussion on the devaluing experiences and 'non' experiences of many users. The need is not only for resources and trained staff to develop initiatives with adults now, but also to ensure that children with learning difficulties had opportunities and experiences which empowered them to make the most of their lives as they grew up.

Insights from group members' experiences

Other examples of self development and advocacy groups both in other areas of East Sussex Social Services and voluntary agencies were described by participants, but it was clear that while there was for example, in East Sussex Social Services a general policy and concern about increasing and developing user participation and involvement, the methods used, and the extent to which this was happening, depended greatly on the initiatives and enthusiasm of staff in particular areas, and their ability and skills in facilitating user groups. Related to this, the question of the appropriateness of members of staff of day, and more particularly residential settings facilitating groups was considered. While their knowledge of, and relationships with users could be very positive factors, together with their cognisance of the service, against this was the need for them to be objective and able to be critical of services, if they were to enable and support users in feeling free to comment or complain.

A staff facilitator of such a group thought that the development of the confidence of users to make suggestions, requests and complaints was part of the staff role, in a relationship of trust. Another participant described the successful progress of two groups in Eastbourne where outside facilitators were used. These were in residential settings where constraints on users could be considerable. The possibility of staff from different establishments facilitating groups was thought to be a good compromise.

There was general agreement among participants on the need for advocacy groups across the statutory and voluntary sectors, and that an important aim of such groups must be to seek to empower users to facilitate and run these groups themselves. Not everyone would choose or necessarily be able to do this, but as in all groups, there were usually one or two people with interest and potential skills.

User participants were the best advocates of groups already in existence, describing ways in which they had been able to make choices about where to live, educational and training courses to take, interests to pursue, and greater confidence in standing up for themselves. One participant said that a group had helped her and others to handle disputes and conflicts that inevitably arose between users at times.

Another user raised the problem of difficulties with parents/carers as a result of increased independence and freedom of choice, and there was a general acknowledgement of problems of parental resistance to advocacy groups resulting from protective anxiety and concern about loss of control in the face of emerging autonomy. The need to work together with parents and carers towards change, and the acceptance of their sons and daughters as adults with rights and responsibilities was strongly endorsed.

The move towards greater integration and involvement in the community, and to some extent away from service provision, afforded users the opportunities and experiences to make informed choices about life styles, and the importance of this could not be over emphasised. In order to make informed choices, you needed to know what choices there were. In relation to this a user pointed out that this often resulted in parents also having to make choices about what sort of relationship they wanted with their offspring!

Other less positive experiences of users were discussed, such as unfilled hopes and expectations in relation to job opportunities. One user told of how he worked side by side with another person on the same job, but the latter was paid and he was not. Service providers involved in trying to negotiate for employment talked of the difficulties in finding work, and even when a job was available frequently no account was taken of an individual's particular interests and aptitudes.

With regard to service provision, emphasis was placed on the fact that services must be committed to what individuals need and want, rather than planning services to fit people into. It was essential that user led services were developed, which involved a sharing of power and control. This meant changes in concepts and ideas about management, and the control of resources. It also had considerable implications for the roles of staff providing services.

The meaning of empowerment

Additionally, if the words 'users first', 'participation', 'user involvement', 'choice', were to mean anything, they must be about open ended questions being asked of users, not, 'do you want this or that' which limited choices. It was important that questions should be about life chances and opportunities, and not simply about service provision.

Finally, if real change was to occur, bearing in mind the time needed for users to become genuinely empowered, this meant resources, training and support for all involved. There was also no way that users could become empowered if the professional staff involved felt, and were, disempowered themselves.

8 Involving people with physical disabilities

Group leader: Val Richards
Brighton and Hove Federation for the Disabled
Reporter: Michael Cahill

In working towards user-led services in physical disability information, advocacy, resources, accessibility and flexibility were the key issues identified by the group

Information needs

Information has to be available to those people who need it and this means that it should not lie undisturbed in a social worker's filing cabinet. Information belongs to the person who needs it. Too often people are not aware of relevant information. For example, the Independent Living Fund has been of immense help to those disabled people who have heard of it and used it but there are many others who could have used it but were unaware of its existence. The same is true of the Family Fund for expenses in connection with disabled children. There are various ways in which information can be disseminated and directories are very useful. A local example identified by the group was Missing Links for the Brighton and Hove district which lists over 120 organisations in a loose leaf binder.

Information is also required on what people want and the needs assessment requirements laid on Health Authorities and Social Services Departments by the NHS and Community Care Act were welcomed as a step forward. Information should be regarded as a right, and a right which is essential, not just to be able to obtain appropriate health and social services but in order to be able to participate in the wider community.

Resource centres were identified as important for the gaining of skills and furthering education. They can also help facilitate when disabled people have problems in using services and gaining information. Centres for Employment and Disabled Living Centres are likewise very important in helping people live a fuller life. Resource centres can be either statutory or voluntary and are needed both to provide information, advice, assistance and counselling and also help to carers, partners and parents.

Accessibility

In order to participate in our society it was recognised that physically disabled people need accessibility. It is the physical environment that has the greatest impact on people with physical impairments. Accessibility means that shops, pubs, cinemas, universities – you name it- should be able to be used by disabled people. Public transport as well – there are not very many buses which can take wheelchairs but this is not because they have not been invented. If public transport was accessible then there would be benefits for non-disabled people like parents of small children who would be able to get their pushchairs and shopping on the bus without difficulty.

Naturally it is not a lot of use having fully accessible transport if it is infrequent and expensive. There was a recognition that although fully accessible transport will only be available for a small number of people as with various community transport and dial-a-ride schemes the bus companies could improve the accessibility of buses by investing in vehicles with low steps and other aids for people with mobility problems. Bus conductors had performed a useful service in the past making entry and exit to a bus less stressful for some passengers.

Much more needs to be done in making buses user friendly: non-slip handrails, contrasting colour edges to steps, non-slip flooring and low level bell pushes.

Empowerment

If empowerment is to mean anything in the move to bring about user-led services then the group felt that it should result in physically disabled people being given a much greater say in how money is spent on their services. This could mean that money is given direct to them so that they can organise their own package of care, as is being done by some local authorities in England and Wales. The services people receive should not depend on where they live or the concessions of their local authority. Community care can only work successfully if disabled people are fully involved in the assessment procedure. Under Section 3 of the Disabled Persons Act disabled people or their authorised representatives have the right to make representations about their community care needs during the assessment procedure. Section 1 and Section 2 set up an advocacy system. Often the care offered by statutory services can be too inflexible for disabled people as they are organised to suit the convenience of staff. Services need to become more flexible in the future.

It was argued that the distinction between users and professionals should be questioned. It is time for some professionals to 'come out of the closet' and admit that they too have disabilities and that they are users of services or have been in the past. It was recognised that although these are small measures compared with the size of the problems confronting disabled people – particularly discrimination in employment – they are nevertheless important steps forward in gaining more power.

9 Involving carers

Group leader: Penny Kocher, Carers Development Officer
East Sussex Care for the Carers Council
Reporter: Peter Frost

As an introduction to the workshops the role of carers in East Sussex and their involvement in service planning by statutory agencies was described.

Recognition of the role of carers in East Sussex

The Government's white paper "Caring for People" acknowledges that "the reality is that most care is provided by family, friends and neighbours". This has been recognised in East Sussex to the extent that Carers have a formal voice across the county through a well-established system of local forums and district development groups. This "Voice for Carers" has enabled carers to have a collective and therefore stronger voice. The Forums play an important role in consultation, both when representatives from various agencies and elected members are invited to attend, and when Forum members represent carers' views on various planning groups.

There is therefore a well established structure for involving carers in East Sussex. In a more recent development carers have become directly involved in the formulation of the community care plan. Strategy Groups for Carers have been set up to be responsible for writing the section of the Plan related to carers.

As well as the specific Strategy Groups for Carers another way of involving carers has been through membership of other Strategy Groups. In this way carers have a voice in the planning process for specific client groups including children, people with physical disabilities, people with learning difficulties, people with mental health problems and elderly people.

The last few years have therefore seen a major development in terms of involving carers at all levels in the county.

Problems of involving carers

As well as discussing the ways in which carers have become involved the carers discussion group focused on some of the issues relating to this involvement. These included the empowerment of carers, the costs of involvement and the problems of contacting and representing the vast numbers of carers in the area.

A major part of empowerment for carers relates to the pressure that they can exert within the political process. While there have always been large numbers of carers their voice has been weak and their impact limited. Carers are by definition very tied to their situation and have little time and energy to become involved. Above all they are scattered and rarely come together as a group or movement. Recent experience however has demonstrated that policies can be challenged given the exercise of group pressure. An example in East Sussex has been the reversal of the proposed policy to charge parents for respite care for children with special needs. In this case a meeting of some one hundred parents played a major part in changing policy. The problem for carers is, however, how to exert such pressure without placing impossible burdens on carers themselves. The formation of carers pressure groups starting with one for parents of children with special needs has been suggested as a way of maintaining and increasing the voice of carers. Such a group could also seek to influence the allocation decisions of commissioners at county and local level.

A second aspect of empowerment to emerge was the key role of information. In East Sussex the collection of basic information on who gets what and how much in terms of basic services has had a major impact. The myth of community care support can be exposed by a simple statistic, for example that only 40% of carers have any support in the home and that the average amount for those who do is only 2 hours a week. Information on the level of provision can also be a powerful force in giving carers a voice. This information has been lacking even in recent years and it is difficult to say exactly how many carers there are or what services are available.

One approach reported in East Sussex has been the establishment of a set of minimum standards of support for carers. For example the proposal that all carers should be entitled to at least one weeks break a year may represent a very low level of support but is a major challenge to existing services. The setting of standards leads to the notion of rights for carers. For example should carers be enabled to return to work if they wish? Thus equal opportunities legislation can be used to empower carers.

Empowerment also relates to the development from criticism to negotiation. Carers are now in a situation of of putting forward specific proposals or being involved in groups making key decisions. Such a role will require new skills and training if carers are to be effective.

The discussion groups also focused on the issue of the cost of becoming involved. For a carer to attend a meeting involves a number of costs. These include the money costs of attending but also of replacing their own care. Many carers receive so little relief that to use the precious two or three hours they have is too costly. In many cases other priorities must come first, for example doing the shopping or simply having a break. These problems can be overcome by the extra provision of a sitter and payment of expenses. When there are two carers, for example two parents of a child with special needs, the decision to become involved will have a direct impact on the other carer. This may inhibit carers taking a direct role or even attending meetings.

Another major issue was identified as the emotional cost of being involved in the planning or negotiating process. Carers are so closely involved in their situation that issues of improved support or better standards are very important indeed. This emotional cost is especially high when services are being cut or reduced. To have the responsibility of arguing for a service which may be a matter of survival for a group of carers is often a very great burden indeed. In some cases this problem can be helped by the use of ex carers in key roles. They still have the vital experience and knowledge but the immediate pressure will have been reduced.

The final major problem raised was that of contacting and involving the vast number of carers in a county like East Sussex. Carers groups and forums as yet reach a small minority of carers.

10 User led services in mental health

Group leader: Marion Beeforth, Brighton Insight
Reporter: Valerie Williamson

Users and service providers were more or less equally represented in these workshops which facilitated the setting of user led agendas. However the success with which this was achieved depended to a considerable extent on the skill of the group leader who devoted the first 15 minutes of each session to pair group discussion among the participants exploring the background to their individual interests in mental health services and learning about one another. This activity 'broke the ice' and helped dissipate tension. Group members were also assured that confidences would be respected and general issues not personal details incorporated in the report. If users are to be involved in meaningful discussions about needs and related service provision, whether at conferences such as this or in other consultative fora, such a careful introductory process designed to boost confidence and allay anxiety is essential.

The key issues identified by the groups for further discussion, fell into two main categories:

1 How can users be more effectively involved in the planning and management of their own treatment?

2 How can users be more effectively involved in needs assessment and the planning of service provision?

How can service users be more effectively involved in the planning and management of their treatment?

First and foremost users wish to regain control of their own lives via active participation in their own treatment.

Users first

1 Facilitate informed consent to medication – The strongest feelings were aroused by this issue. The general consensus of the group was not to oppose medication as such , many recognised the potential benefits, but to resist the lack of informed personal choice. It was stressed that users should be told about the potential side effects of drugs and the likely results of neglecting to take their medication and then to have an opportunity to discuss all relevant options. Opinion varied as to how forthcoming staff were in terms of volunteering information, some participants believing that lies were sometimes told.

Sectioned patients were recognised as particularly vulnerable to enforced medication and the proposed introduction of Community Treatment Orders was opposed on these grounds. One user present strongly resented having been previously sectioned and forcibly medicated. Recognising the social unacceptability of his behaviour, he none the less argued for the option of a term of imprisonment.

It was argued that consultants should be more flexible and willing to see how users managed without their drugs, rather than assuming that it was the drugs that kept them well, although it was accepted that withdrawal needs to be managed and supervised. The main concern was that patients invariably had to take the initiative and argue strongly for reduced medication, perhaps because drugs are being used inappropriately to control people rather than for therapeutic reasons.

2 Easier access for users to professional support services in the community.
The principle of community care was endorsed but participants felt strongly that vulnerable users needed speedy access to professional help when they felt the need for it. Users emphasised that families are not always the most appropriate form of support and that perceptions of crisis differed between carers and users. Parents could assume responsibilities inappropriately and users needed to be listened to themselves. From the carers perspective, group members emphasised the strain of coping in a crisis and the need for a quick response from professionals. In one instance a carer had become a user from lack of support. Users charters, as compiled in Brighton and Bromley were supported by those participants familiar with them, as a tool for improving the range and quality of services.

3 Choice of support services – Users expressed a need for better information on the range of services available , such as that provided by the Bromley Health Advice Shop. It was also felt that the range itself could be extended to give a real choice. As somebody to listen was considered very important , counselling services and psychotherapy were highly valued and it was regretted that they were not readily available on the NHS. Local waiting lists for psychotherapy of 6 months were quoted. Self help groups were also viewed as valuable options as users supported each other. Befriending and fostering schemes were considered as an alternative to family care and advocacy schemes seen as an essential aid to informed choice.

4 Training for GPs – GPs are a key resource for users in the community as the point of access to most other statutory services. It was felt however that many GPs lacked the necessary psychiatric training to support mentally ill patients and that as more patients were discharged from hospital they were being placed under increasing pressure and unable to provide the quantity or quality of support needed. Users wanted GPs to have both the time and the counselling skills to involve patients in their treatment, discussing with them the potential side effects of medication for example .

How can users be effectively involved in the planning and management of service provision?

While service providers are keen to incorporate user representation into service planning, it is difficult for users to move beyond their immediate personal concerns about their own treatment until they feel they have established a measure of control at this level. The extent to which users in these two groups were willing to discuss service provision in more general terms is perhaps an encouraging measure of existing achievements.

1 Encourage ex-users to 'come out' – 'Selecting' users was identified as an initial problem. Not only do bureaucratic committee structures frighten some away, but it was argued that the social stigma of mental health encouraged those ex-users who had successfully rehabilitated themselves, to hide any past mental health problems, thus confirming negative stereotypes of mental disability. These attitudes were felt to be most prevalent in rural areas. Those ex-users who had secured employment and were leading stable lives would provide useful role models and would often possess the requisite skills for involvement in planning debates, but risked jeopardising their position if they 'came out'. There was seen to be a moral dilemma here.

2 Encouraging professionals to be more pro-active – To ensure that a wide range of users are made aware of the opportunities to participate in planning, professionals will have to actively publicise them. Putting up posters in GPs waiting rooms was one strategy considered, but it was also argued that recruitment should not just be via health services but also through social services networks. It was further suggested that in view of the continuing stigma of mental illness, it might be easier to attract user representation into planning and management if mental health issues were linked to broader concerns of good health. The common concern that any users recruited might not be truly representative, was answered by the contention that little attempt is made to find representative professionals and that no one seems unduly worried by that.

3 Introduce user empowering processes – Recruiting users into participatory exercises is only a prerequisite first stage in the consultative process. It is important that users feel able to contribute effectively and to participate in agenda setting as well as subsequent debate. The potential of such devices as stake holders conferences, users days and pre-meetings were discussed, together with the potential benefits of collaboration with other disability groups.

Users groups need access to relevant information and training/practice in how to handle professionals especially doctors. Often reluctance to get involved is not because users are unwilling but because they lack the relevant skills. It is also important to meet expenses and even to consider paying consultancy fees. On the basis that professionals are paid for their attendance, a claim was made for equal pay for equal skills. There are particular difficulties about attending meetings in rural areas which might justify a higher level of expenses.

It was recognised that some users might wish to withdraw from participation after a time. It is unrealistic to expect an ongoing commitment from the same people who needed time to get on with their own lives. Statutory authorities also need to realise and allow for the fact that user participation is a stressful occupation for users and that they will not wish to give as much time to it as professional workers who are paid for their involvement.

4) Changing society's attitudes – It was argued that many of the difficulties concerning user involvement refected the problems experienced by professionals in accepting users as people. Attitudes were sometimes patronising and demeaning. An over protective emphasis on caring **for** rather than caring **about**, reflected an unwillingness to accept users as partners. It was argued that users groups could be relied on to regulate themselves in terms of socially acceptable behaviour in the interests of presenting a responsible image, but professionals and non-users needed to be tolerant of each others difficulties.

Overall the message from both morning and afternoon sessions was that users, while acknowledging the existence of their disability and of their need for skilled professional support, wanted to take greater responsibility for their own lives. A number of recommendations suggest how an effective partnership might be developed.

11 Conclusion: the real challenge, the way ahead

Valerie Williamson

As already indicated in the introduction, the central theme to emerge from both the keynote speeches and the workshop debates was user empowerment. Pat Donlan argues that 'empowerment is the business of community care' and the measurement of increased empowered living 'becomes the most significant quality management tool.'

It is also abundantly clear from the preceding pages that empowerment will be challenging. As users become more self-confident and assertive they will raise their expectations in terms of the quantity and quality of services, but recently revealed budgetary allocations for community care make it quite clear that resources will remain severely constrained (1). Indeed the currently proposed review of public sector spending on welfare suggests that the belt may be tightened still further (2). Rationing will become an ever more salient issue and more clearly visible as Social Services Departments become the main budget holders.

Debates will not only surround the classic dilemmas of 'who gets what', who gets anything at all may increasingly become the issue. Local authorities are now compiling eligibility criteria, seeking to prioritise those assessed as in greatest need. In one local scheme, people placed in bands 1-3 will be guaranteed intervention, those in bands 4 and 5 will receive services as resources allow, any shortfall being categorised as unmet need, but those in band 6 'are assessed as not requiring intervention', and as such will not be logged as unmet need (3).

If multi-disciplinary assessments include a strong voice from users and carers, it is unrealistic to assume that there will be a consensus about the nature and extent of need. Research is constantly revealing that peoples' own diagnosis of their problems and prescriptions for their remedy is seldom congruent with that of professional service providers (4).

Users first

Empowered users will be constantly testing providers decisions and a system that really puts them first needs to build in processes for continuous dialogue and negotiation. Decisions will be challenged and conventional service solutions questioned in favour of new and possibly untried remedies.

Service providers, especially in public sector agencies like the National Health Service and Social Services Departments, have traditionally been paternalistic and defensive. Users have been expected to fit in. Complaints are not encouraged and are perceived in a negative light, to be diverted if possible. While models of conciliation are to be supported where there is potential for restoring damaged personal relationships, the whole sphere of complaints needs to be looked at afresh in a more positive vein as a key field for quality assurance strategy. Complaints afford an opportunity to identify problems and understand users' perspectives and priorities with a view to effecting changes in practice.(5)

User empowerment will appear threatening to professional providers as long as they persist in seeing themselves as the legitimate decision makers. Professional expertise should more properly be regarded as fulfilling a vital advisory and facilitating role, informing the likely outcomes of various interventionary strategies and mobilising the necessary resources.

Empowerment can also appear daunting to users. It implies retaining responsibility for their own lives, being well informed and having the self-confidence to assert their views. Some people, as the conference makes clear, will need enabling support, especially those with long term needs, who have been effectively disempowered in the past.

The challenge is considerable for both users and providers, but the reward is to help fashion a humane society where human dignity is respected and, despite resource constraints, choice and opportunity are rights of citizenship available to all.

References

1   Hudson B – Pawn Again – Health Service Journal 26.11.93

2   Count three and chop – Editorial Guardian newspaper 10.2.93

3   Sorensen L – East Sussex Care Management Pilot Project, Evaluation of Users Views. Health and Social Policy Research Centre, University of Brighton 1991

Hutchins K – A Report on the Needs and Views of Physically Disabled People. Health and Social Policy Research Centre, University of Brighton 1993

4   East Sussex County Council Social Services Department – Eligibility Criteria – undated

5   Kaye C and MacManus T – Understanding Complaints – Health Services Journal 23.8.90